WILD FANTASM
FANTASY ART ADULT COLORING BOOK

Copyright © 2019 Vivid Publishers
Illustrated by Chinthaka Herath
Design & layout by Intense Media

All rights reserved. No part of this publication may be reproduced, distributed or transmitted in any form or by any means including photocopying, recording or other electronic or mechanical methods, without the prior written permission of the Publisher/ Chinthaka Herath.

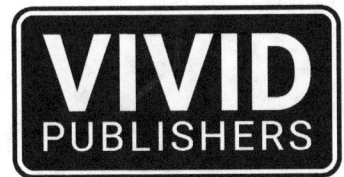

ISBN-13: 9781677068722

INTRODUCTION

Thank you for purchasing 'Wild Fantasm', a fantasy art adult coloring book by Chinthaka Herath. This book features 24 pages of beautiful women combined with animals from the wild.

Open up this book to color away your stress and enter a fantasy world of animals in human form that have been created with a leafy, flowery theme running through them.

All the illustrations are hand drawn by the artist.

You can use any coloring medium from pencils to markers as long as they have a fine tip.

A note on the use of markers: Even though the illustrations are printed one per page, to give additional protection please place a thick paper or cardboard beneath the page you are coloring so that the ink will not bleed through to the next page.

Subscribe at our website to get a FREE 10 Page PDF Sampler 'Fantasy Art Adult Coloring Collection' featuring pages from our three adult coloring books August Reverie 1, 2 and Saga: Fire & Water! Plus, news on discounts, free pages, contests and more!

 www.vividpublishers.com

We would love to see your completed art. You can reach us at:

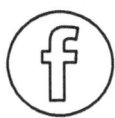 fb.com/VividPublishers

 @VividPublishers

Also, we welcome you to join our Facebook group to share your art, see other colorists' art, enter exciting contests plus more!

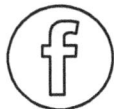 fb.com/groups/VividPublishers

Thank you for your continued support and interest in our adult coloring books. We hope you enjoy coloring the pages as much as we did creating them. Happy Coloring!

CONTENTS

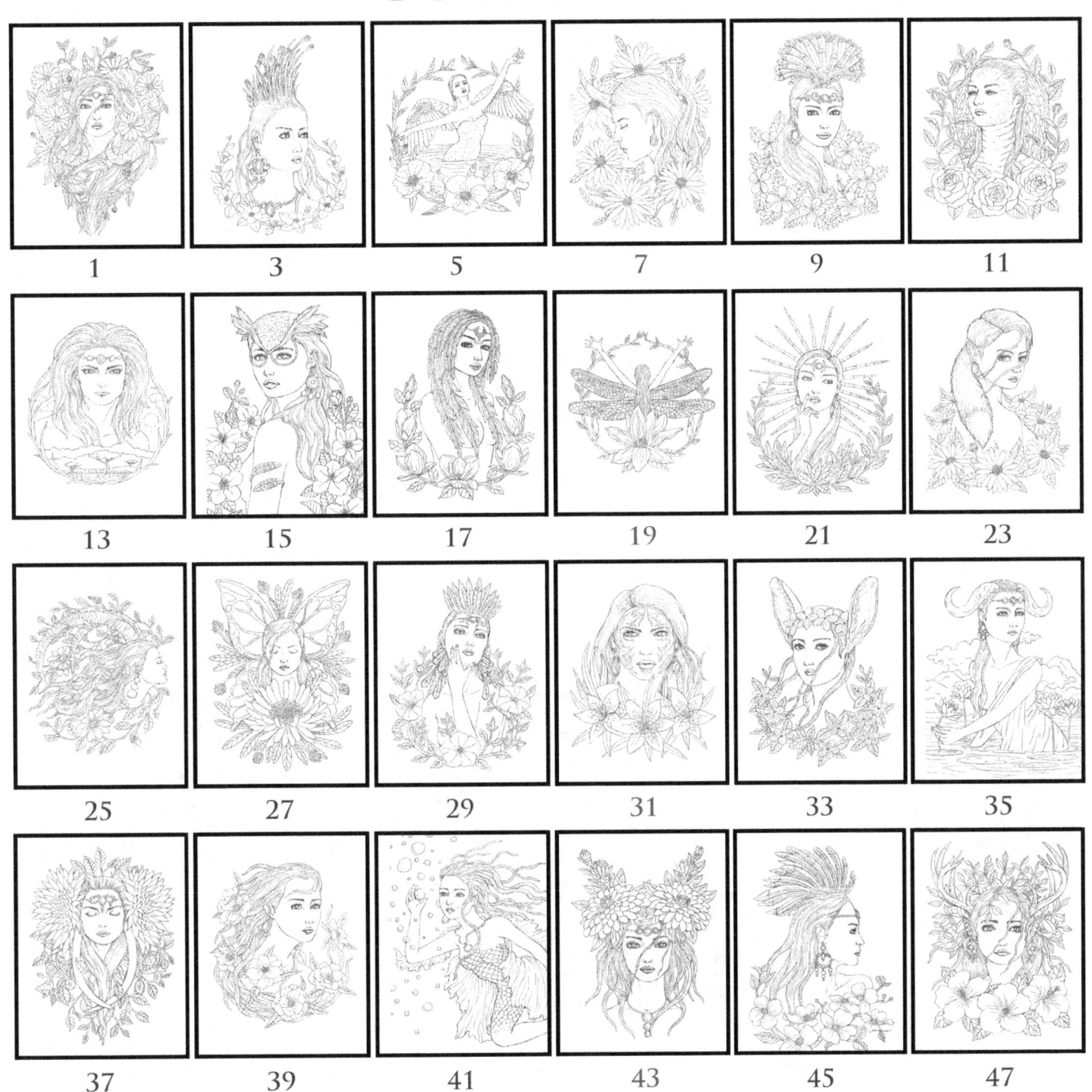

1) MOUFLON   3) SCHALOW'S TURACO   5) SWAN   7) RHINOCEROS
9) AMAZONIAN ROYAL FLYCATCHER   11) COBRA   13) LION
15) GREAT HORNED OWL   17) LONG TAILED WIDOWBIRD
19) DRAGONFLY   21) PORCUPINE   23) FOX   25) CAPRA IBEX
27) BUTTERFLY   29) TUFTED COQUETTE   31) TIGER   33) HARE
35) WATER BUFFALO   37) ELEPHANT   39) HORSE
41) SIAMESE FIGHTING FISH   43) FENNEC FOX   45) HOOPOE   47) DEER

MOUFLON

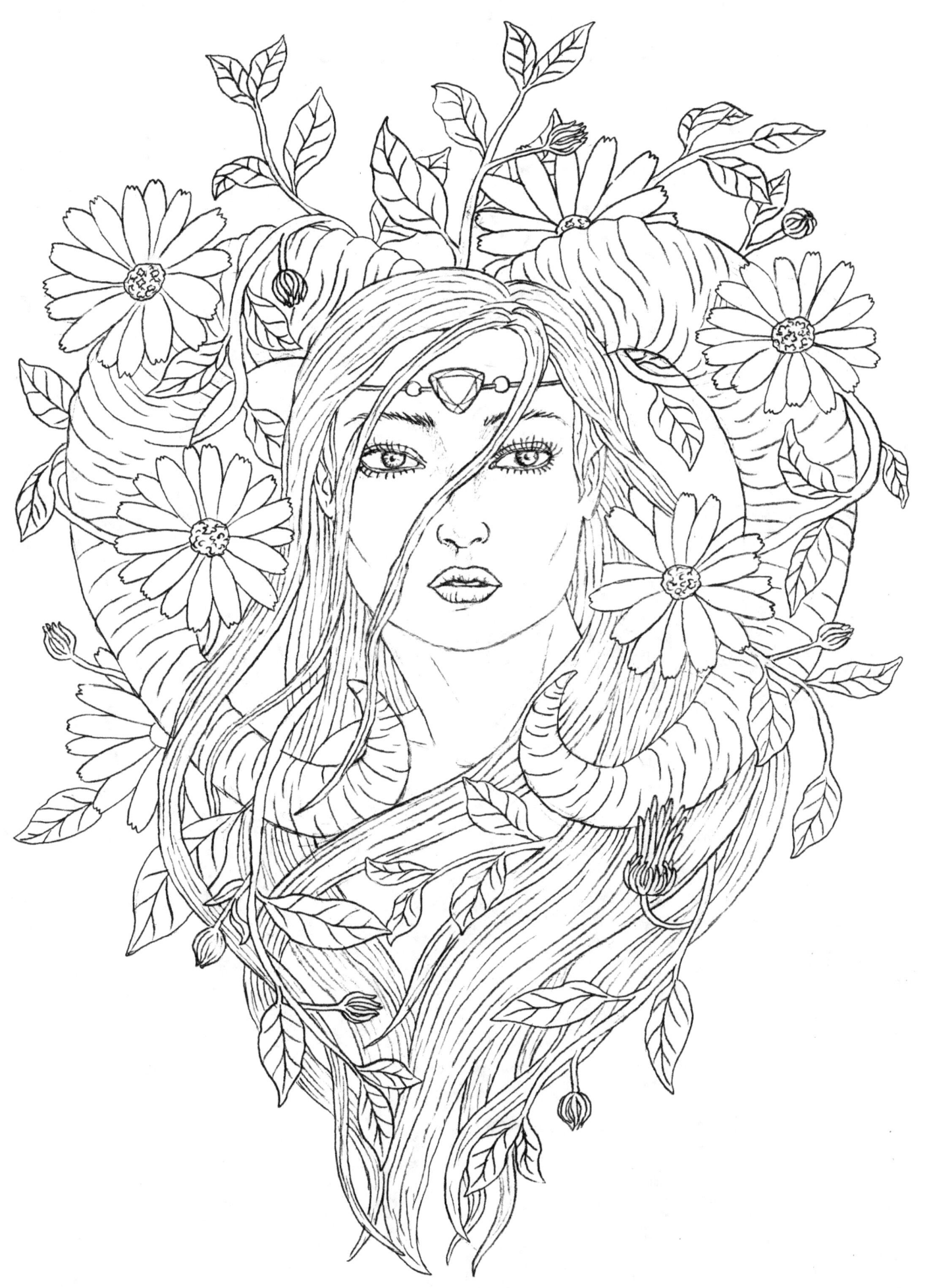

SCHALOW'S TURACO

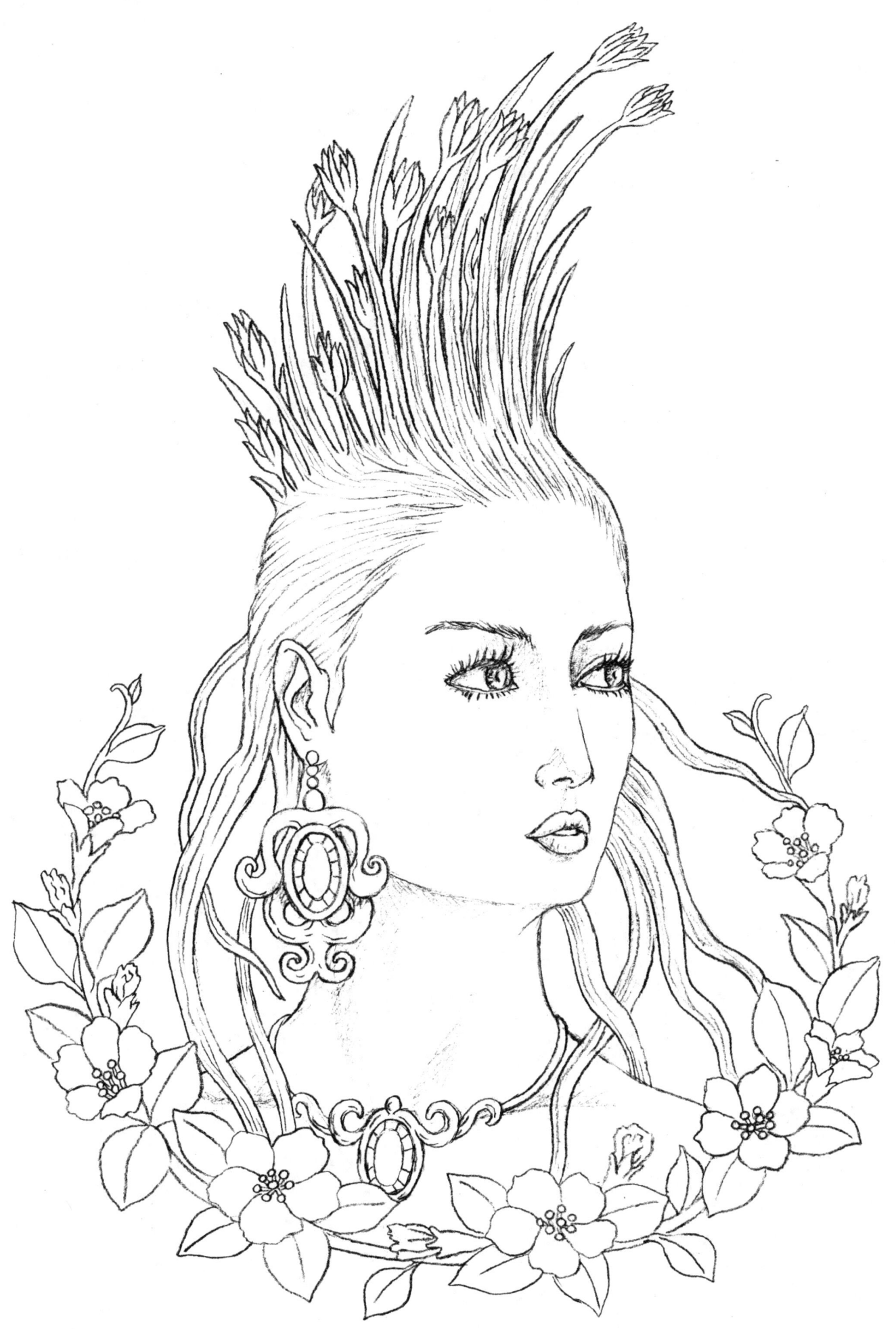

SWAN

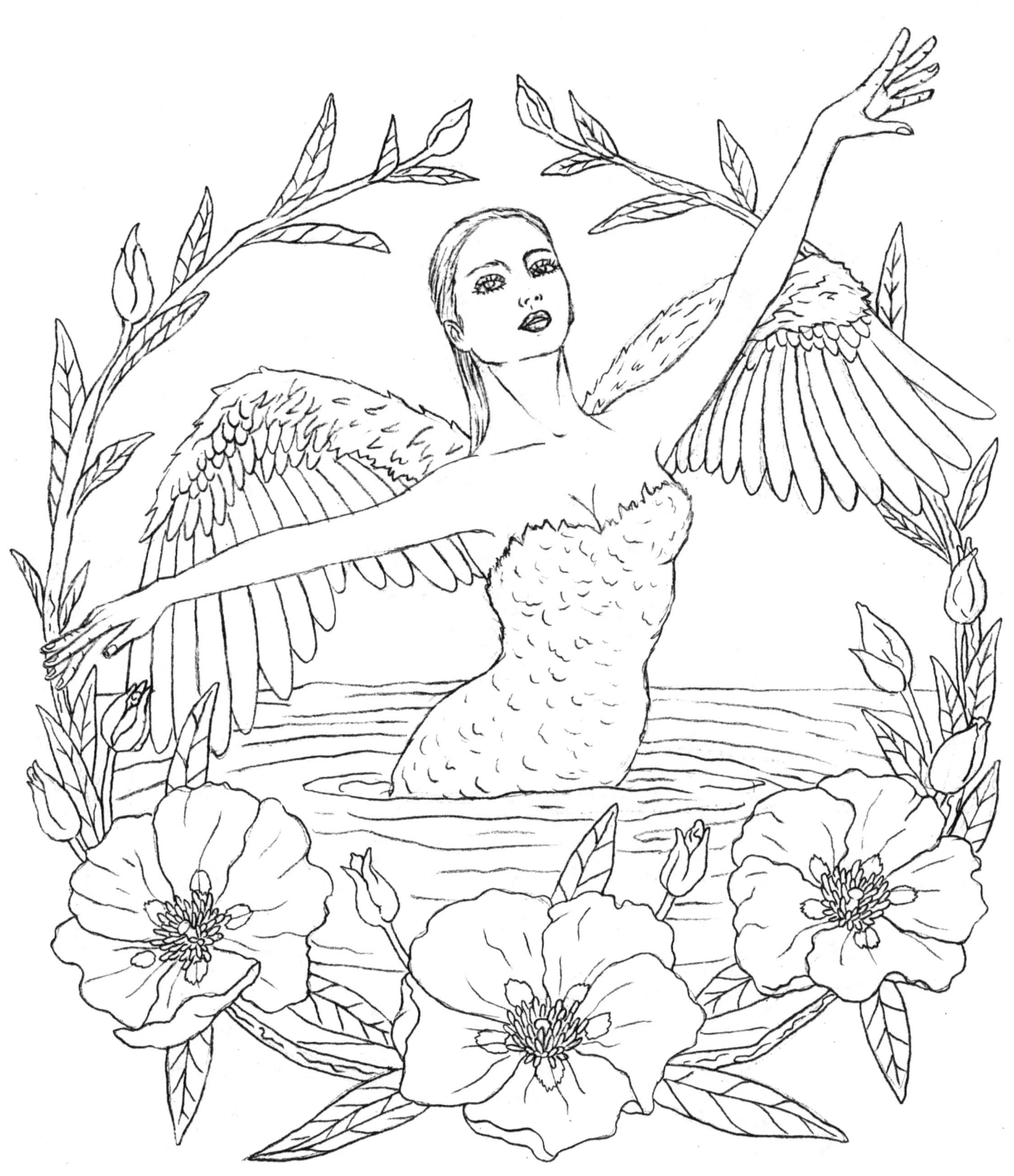

RHINOCEROS

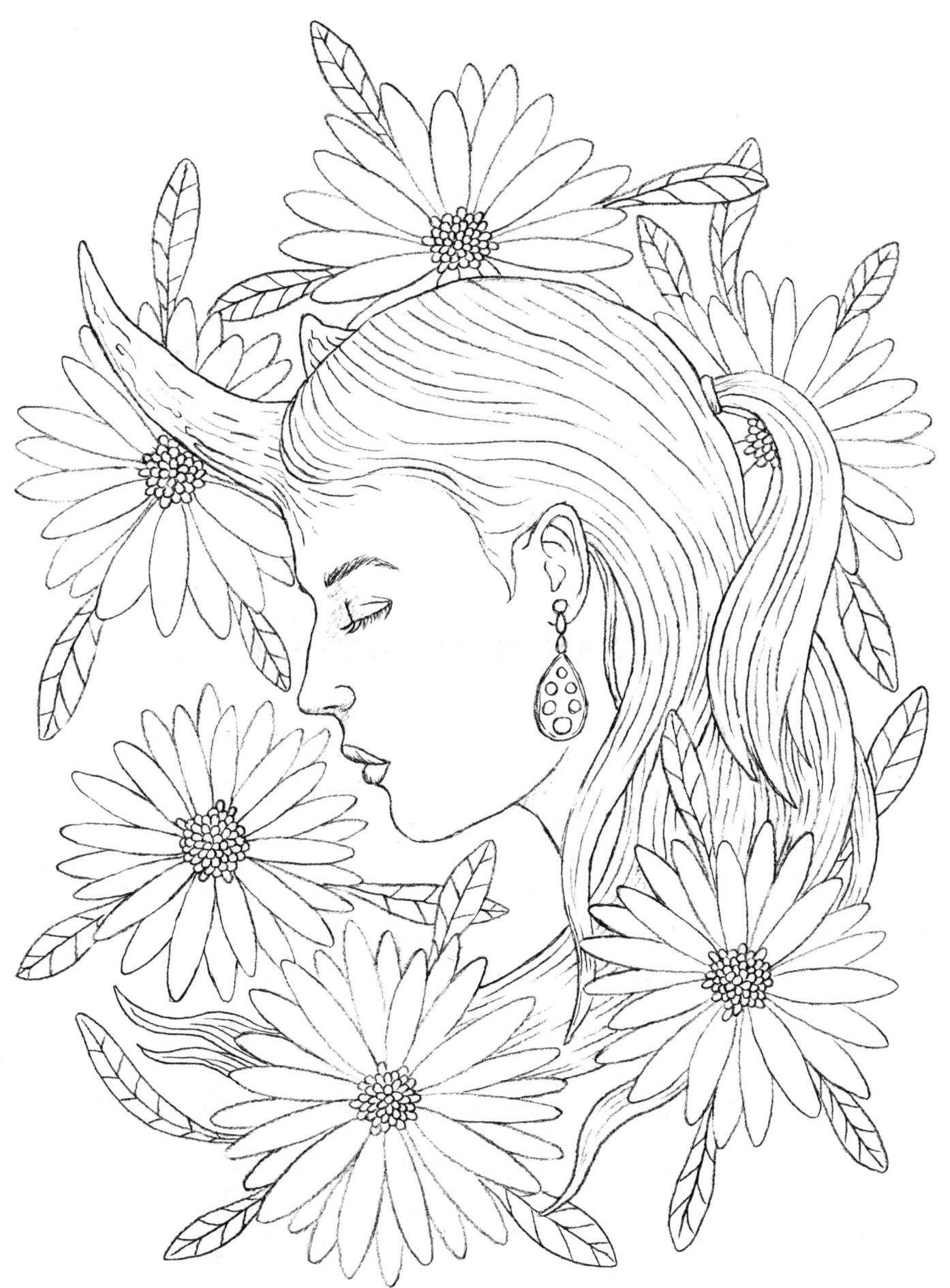

AMAZONIAN ROYAL FLYCATCHER

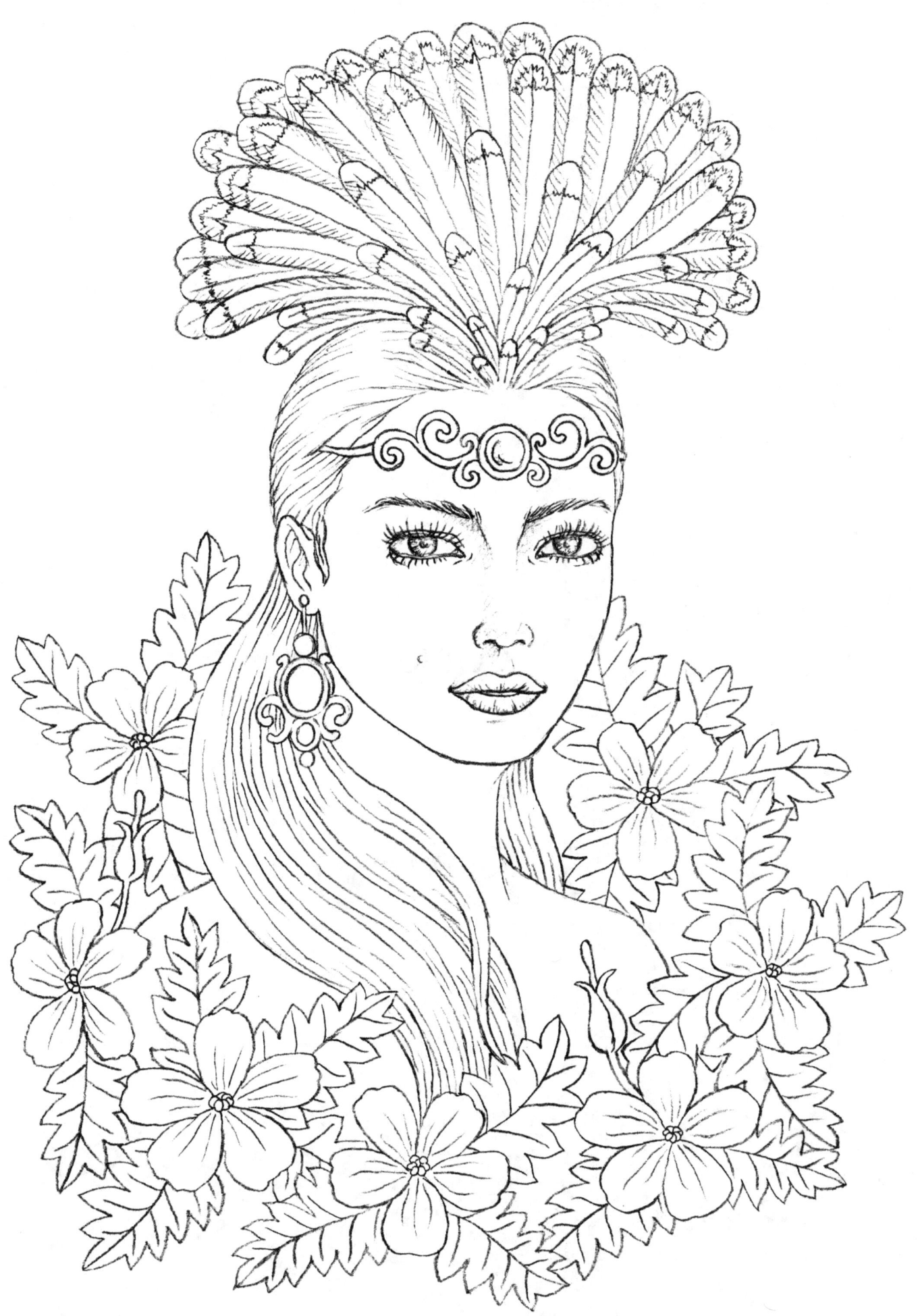

COBRA

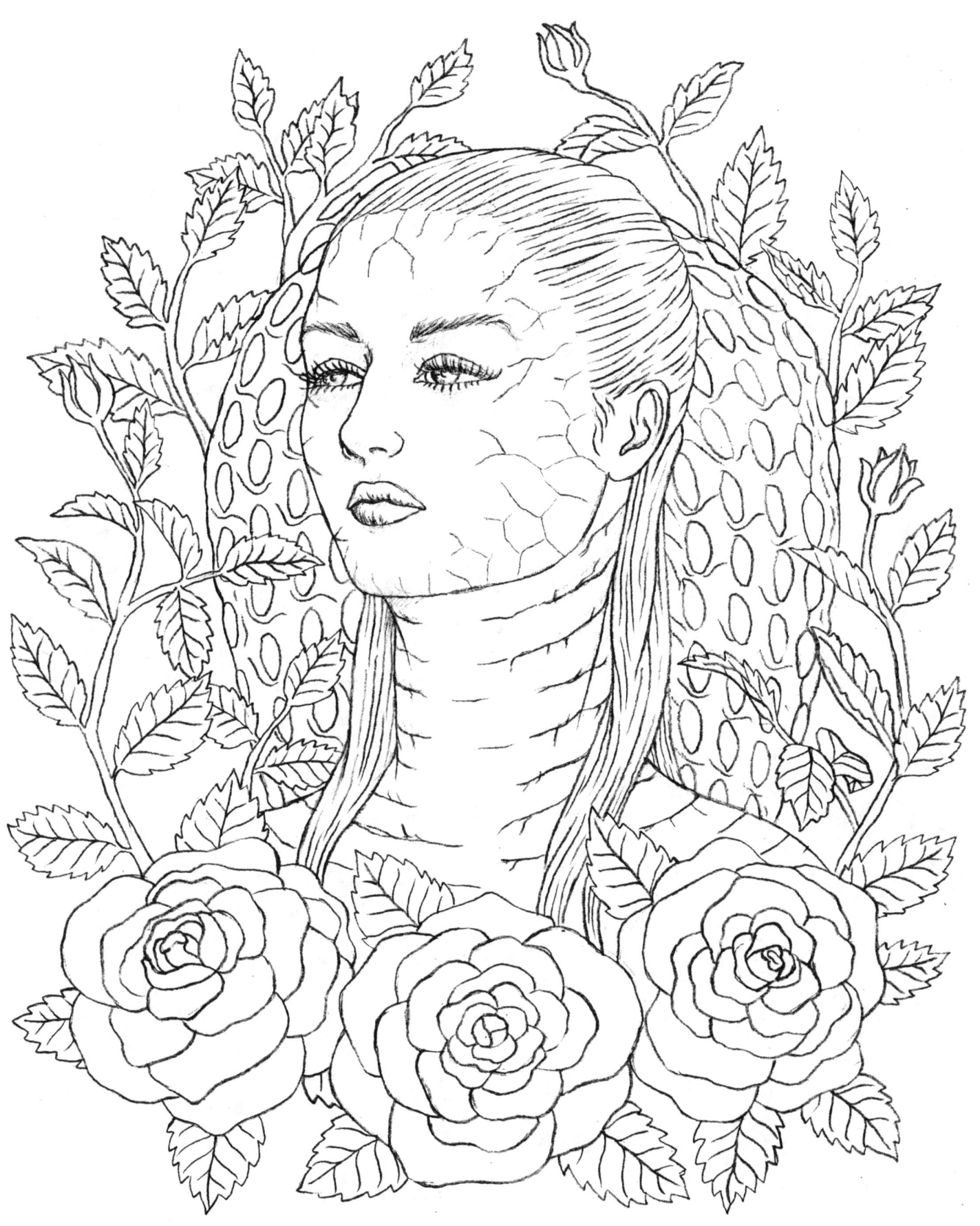

LION

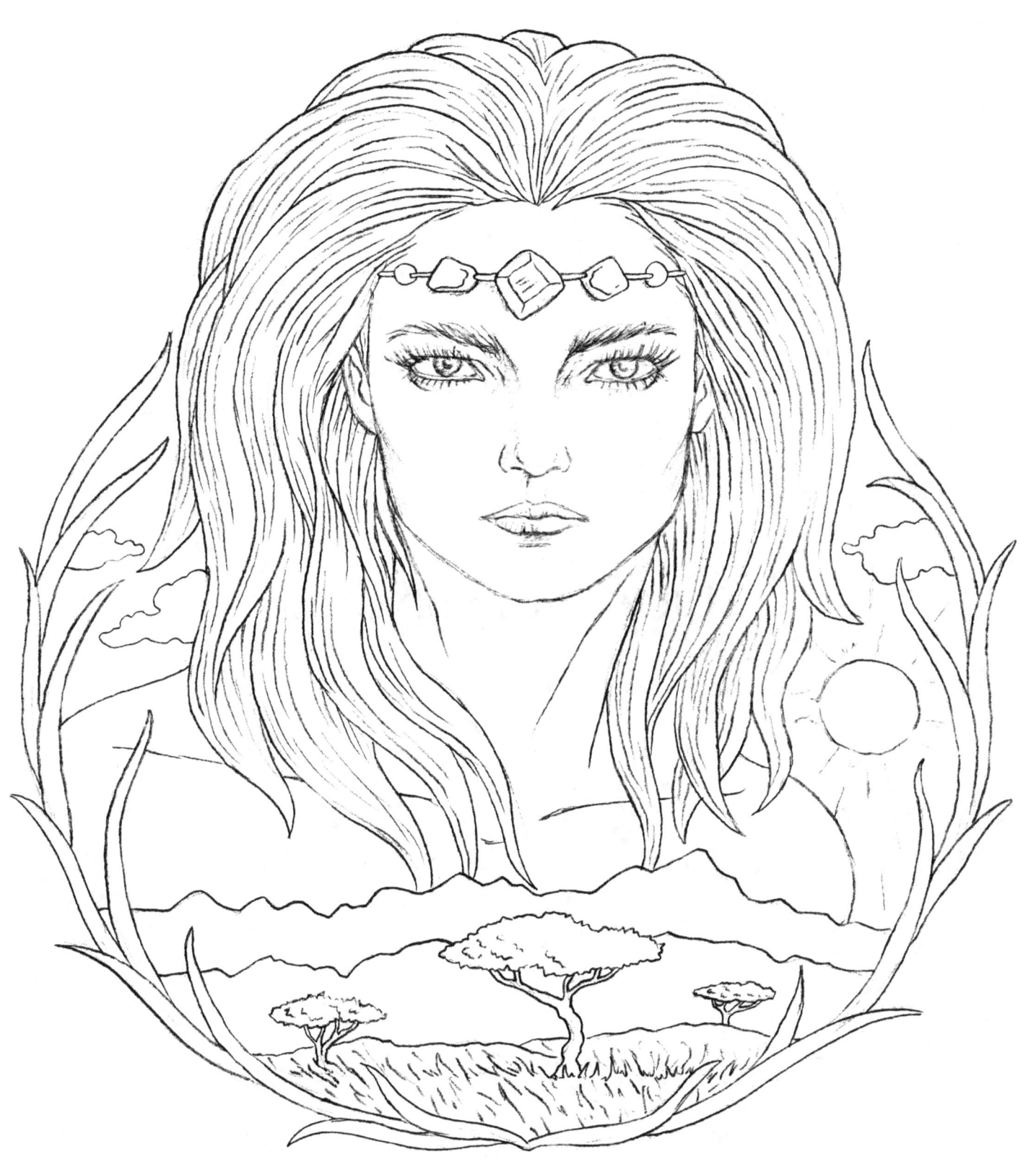

GREAT HORNED OWL

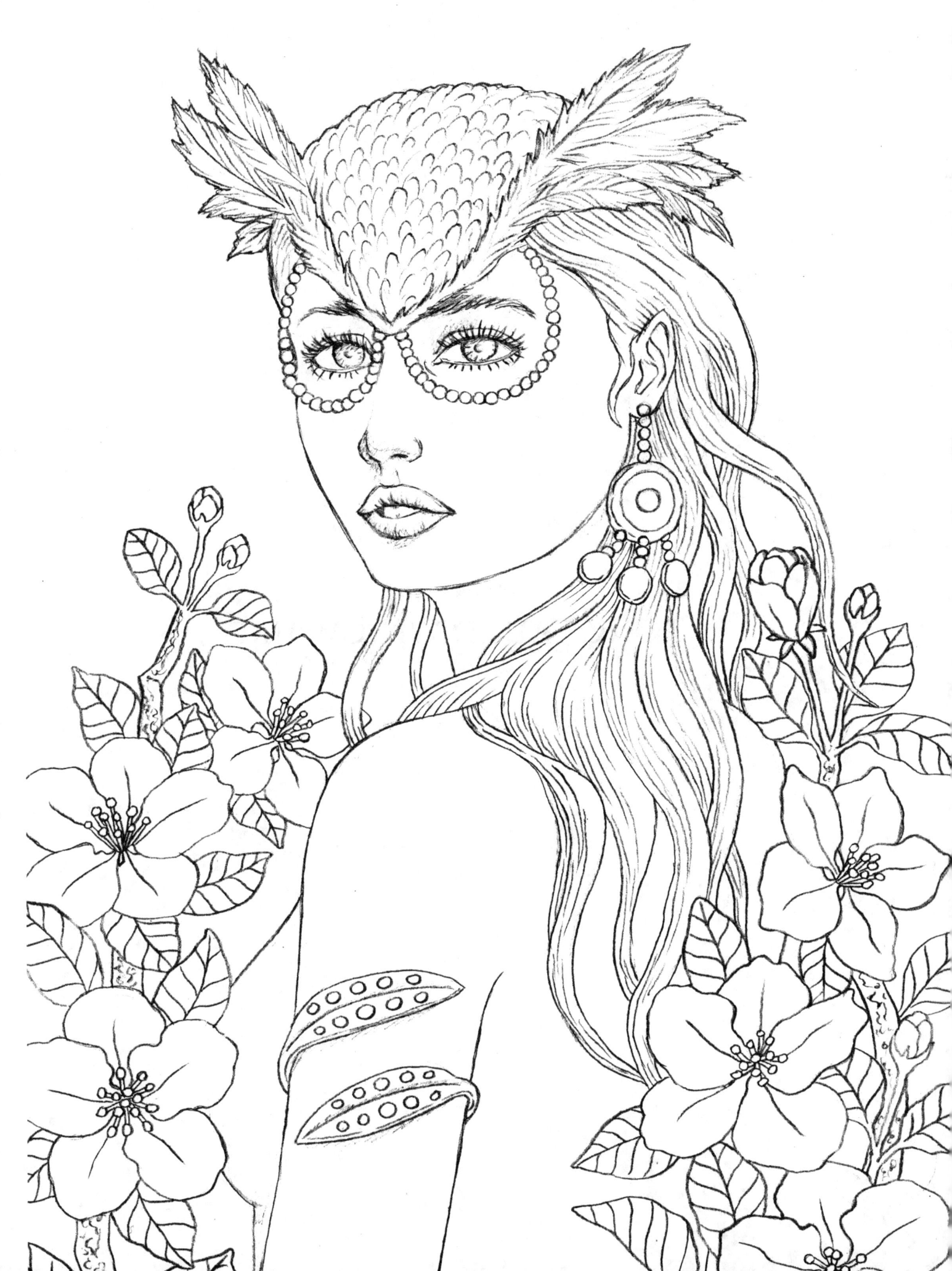

LONG TAILED WIDOWBIRD

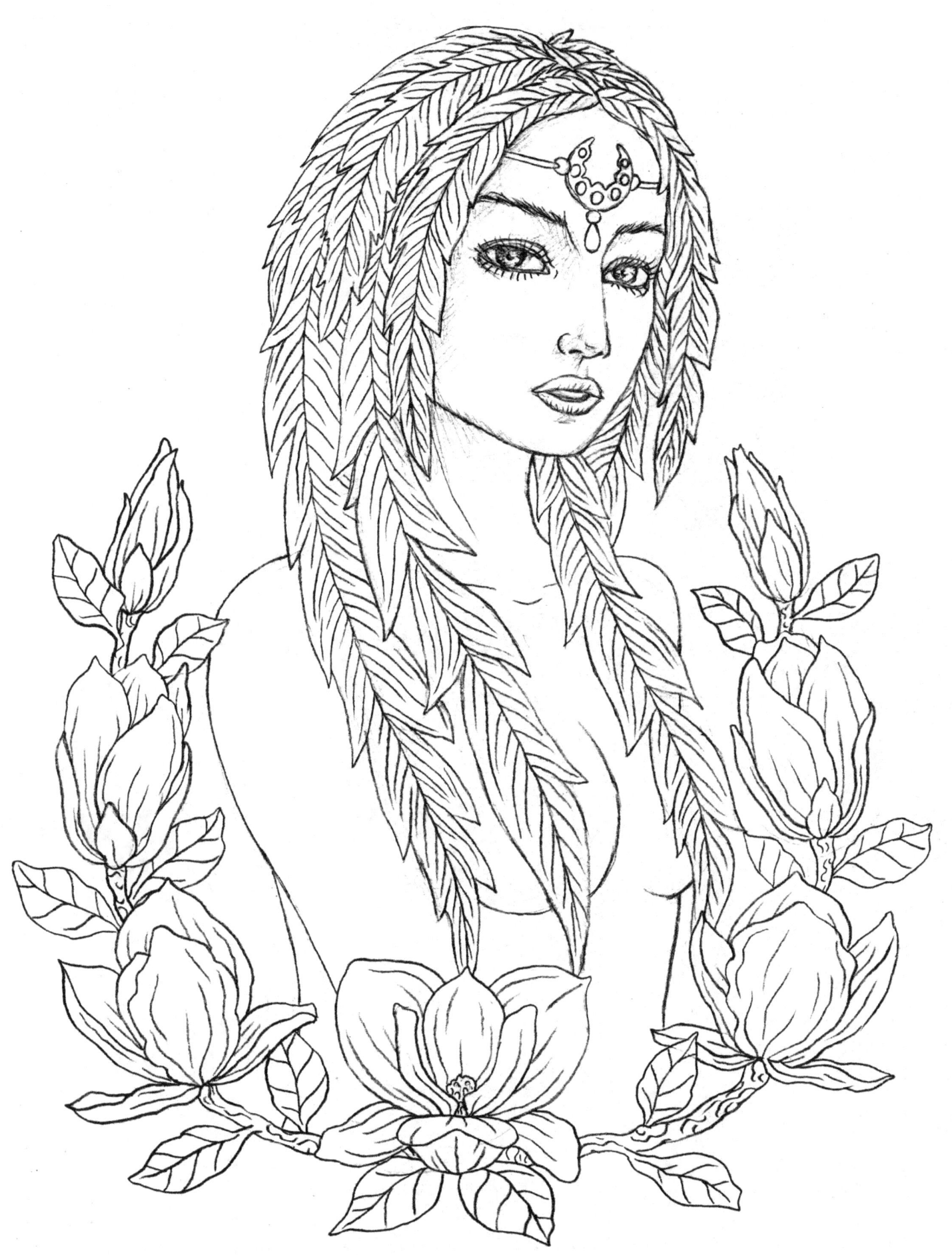

DRAGONFLY

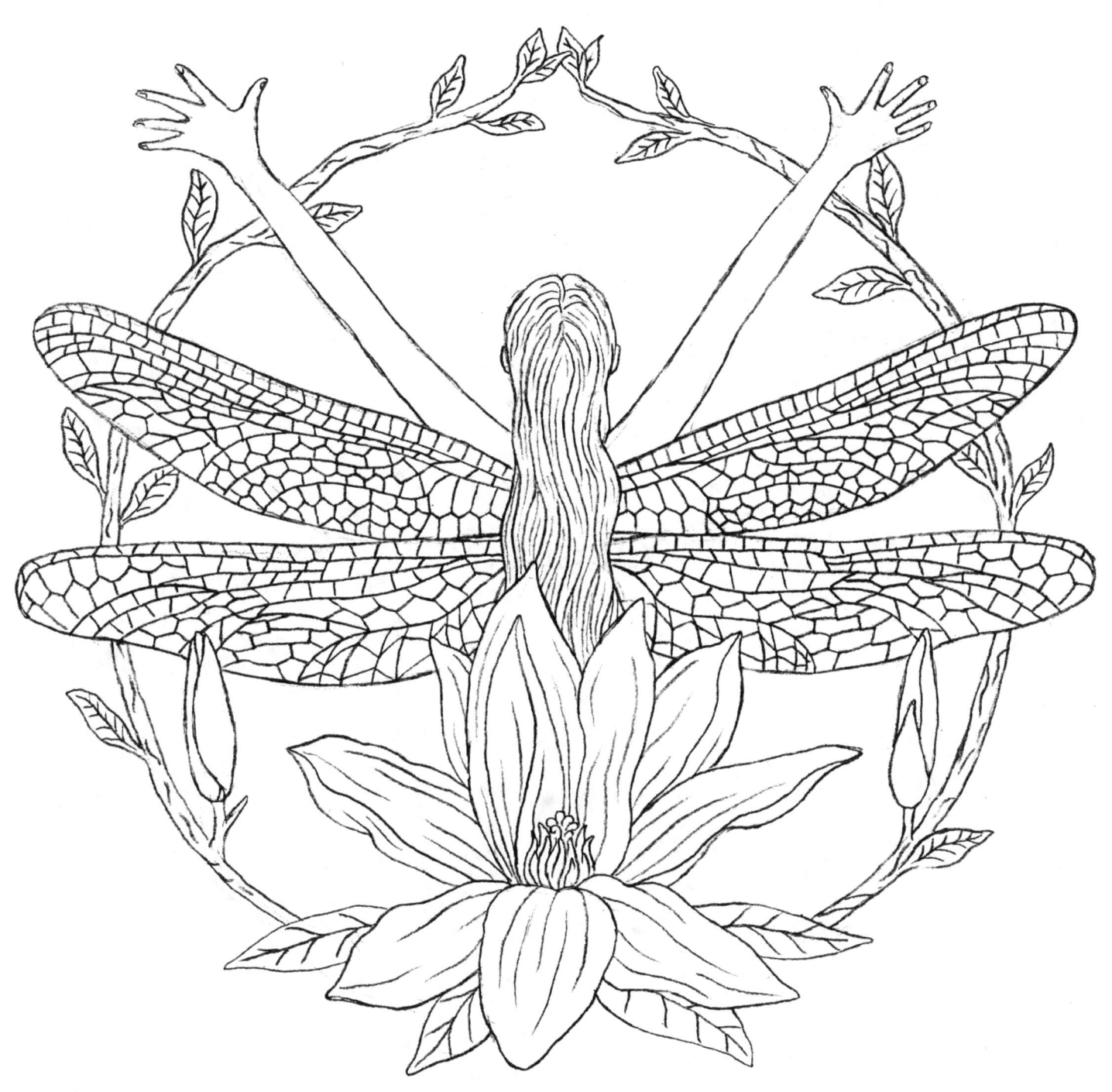

PORCUPINE

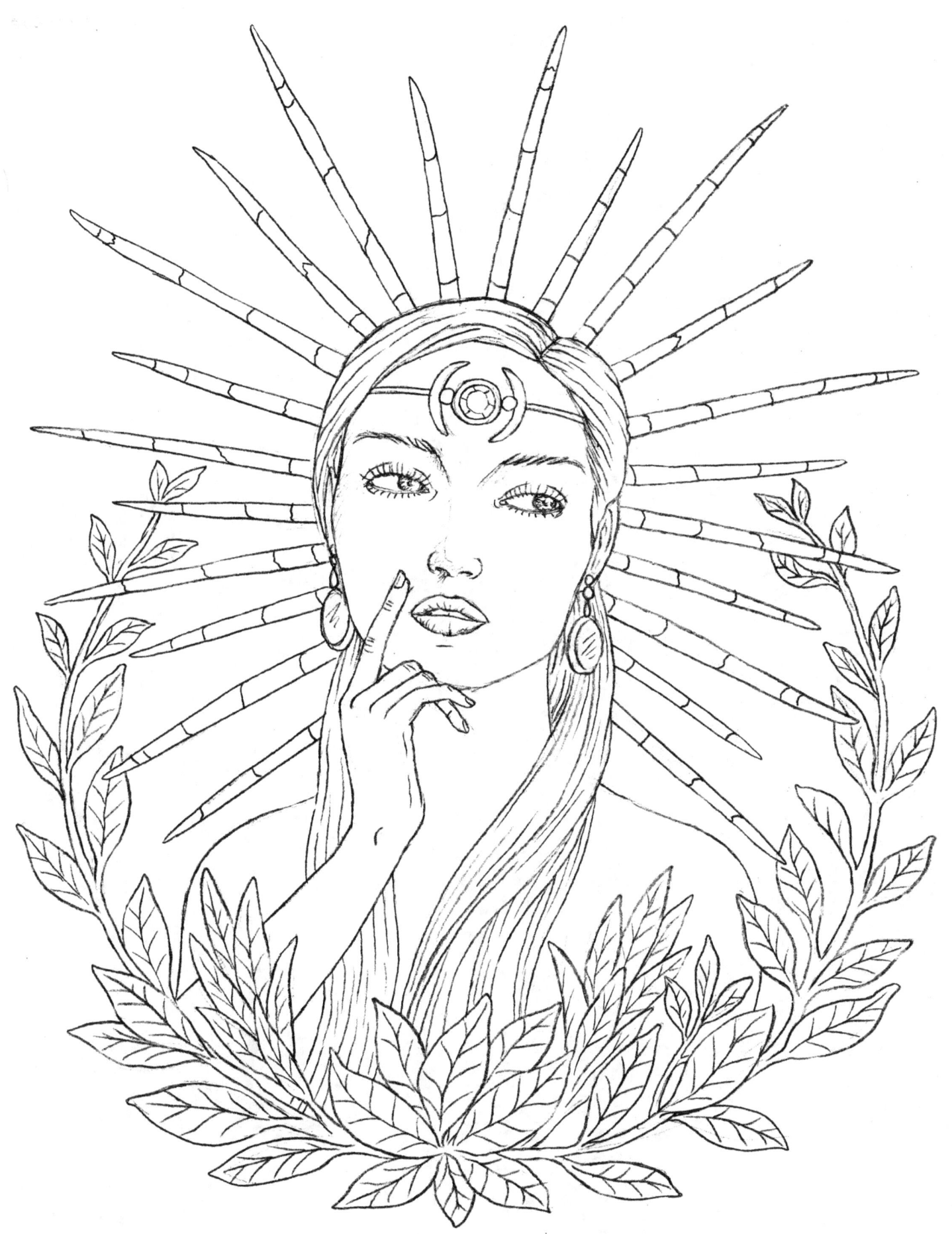

FOX

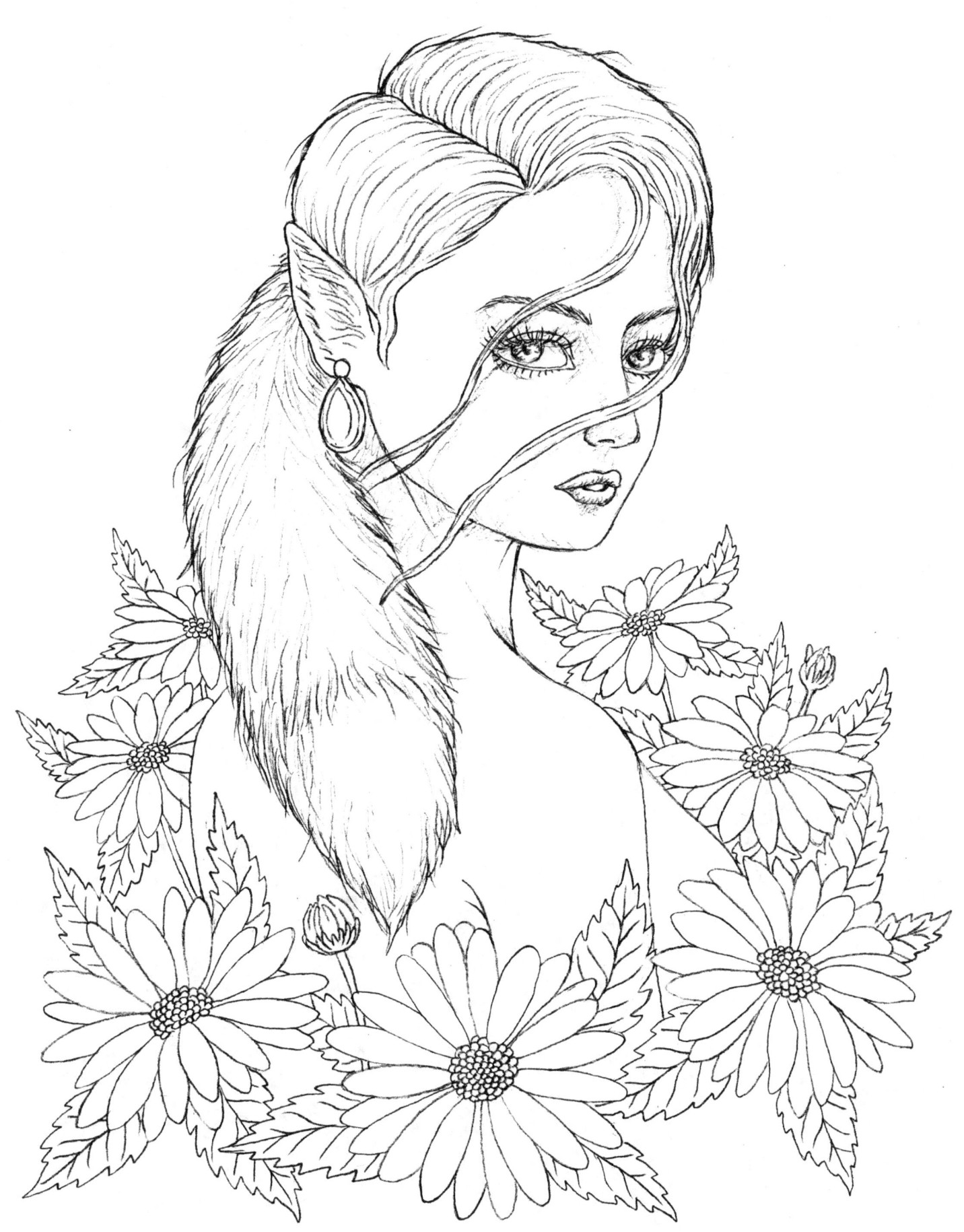

CAPRA IBEX

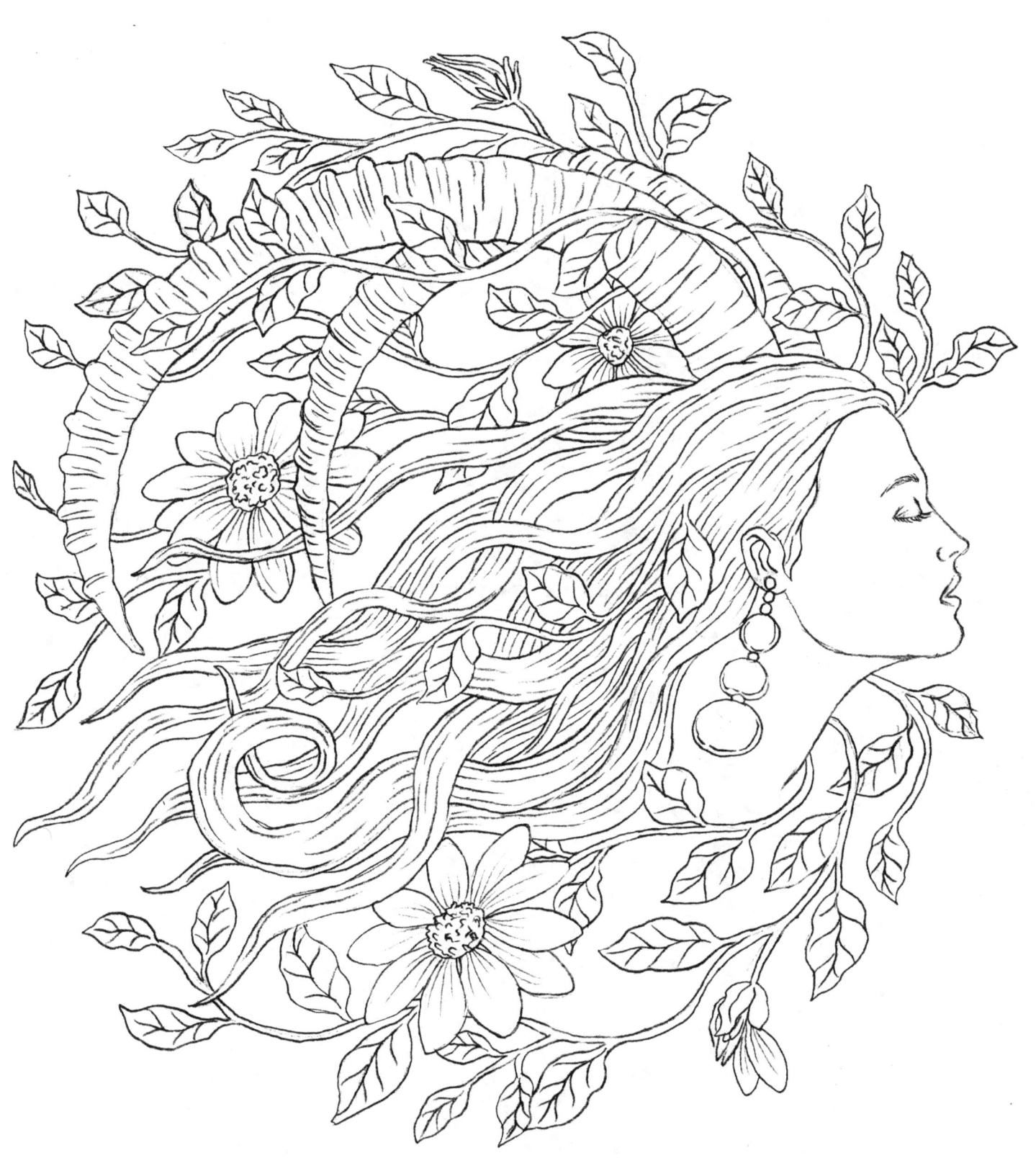

BUTTERFLY

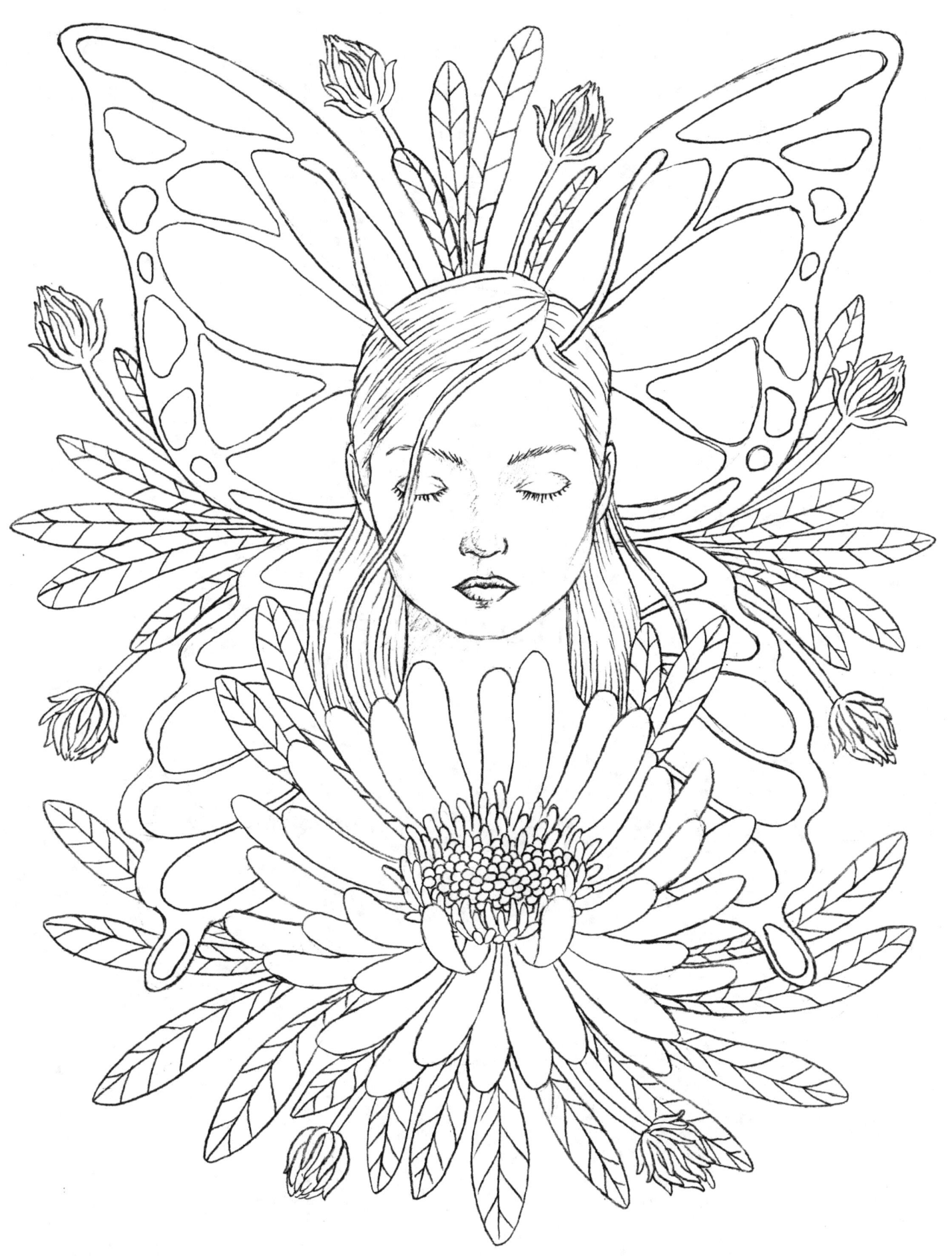

TUFTED COQUETTE

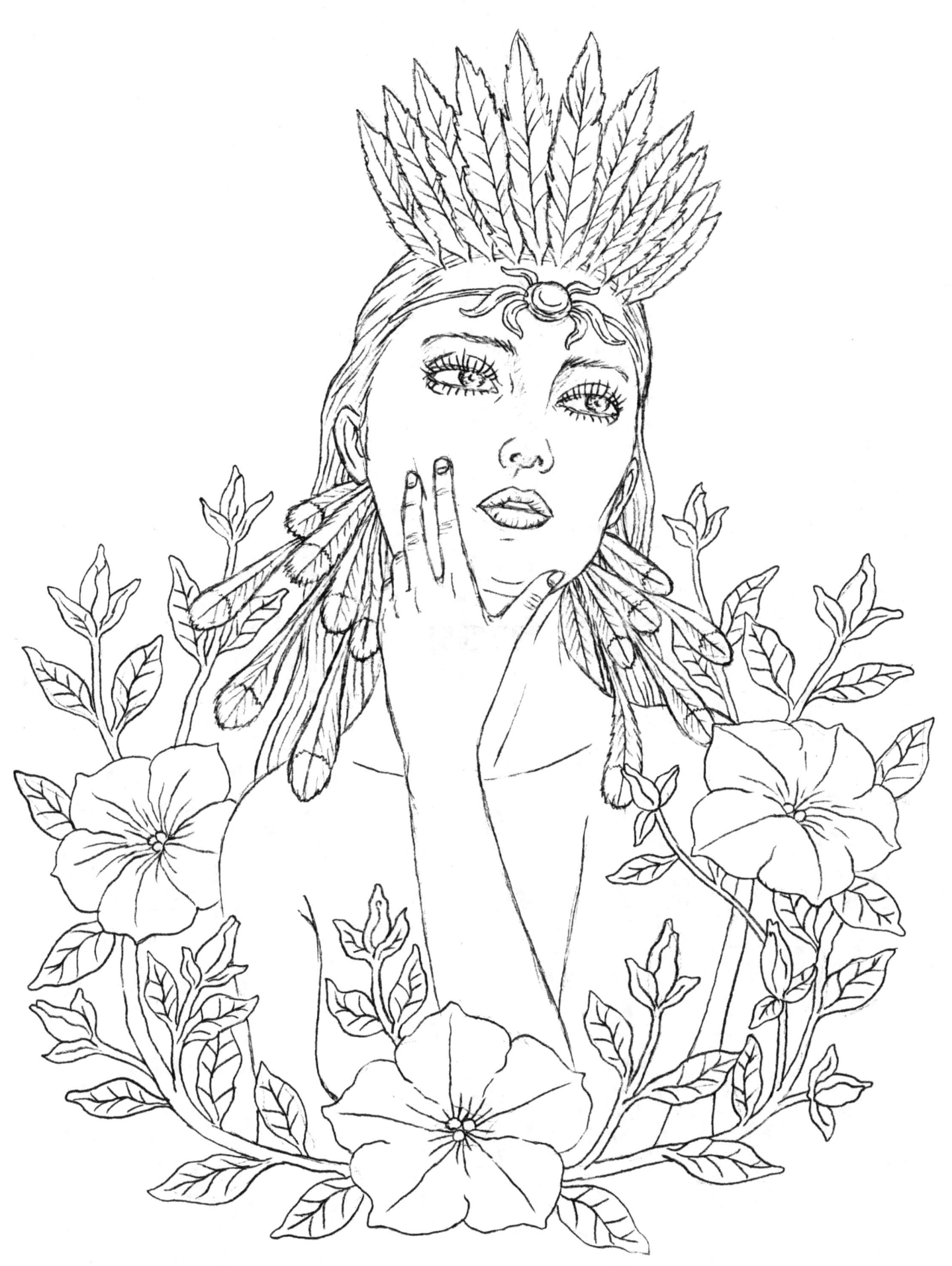

TIGER

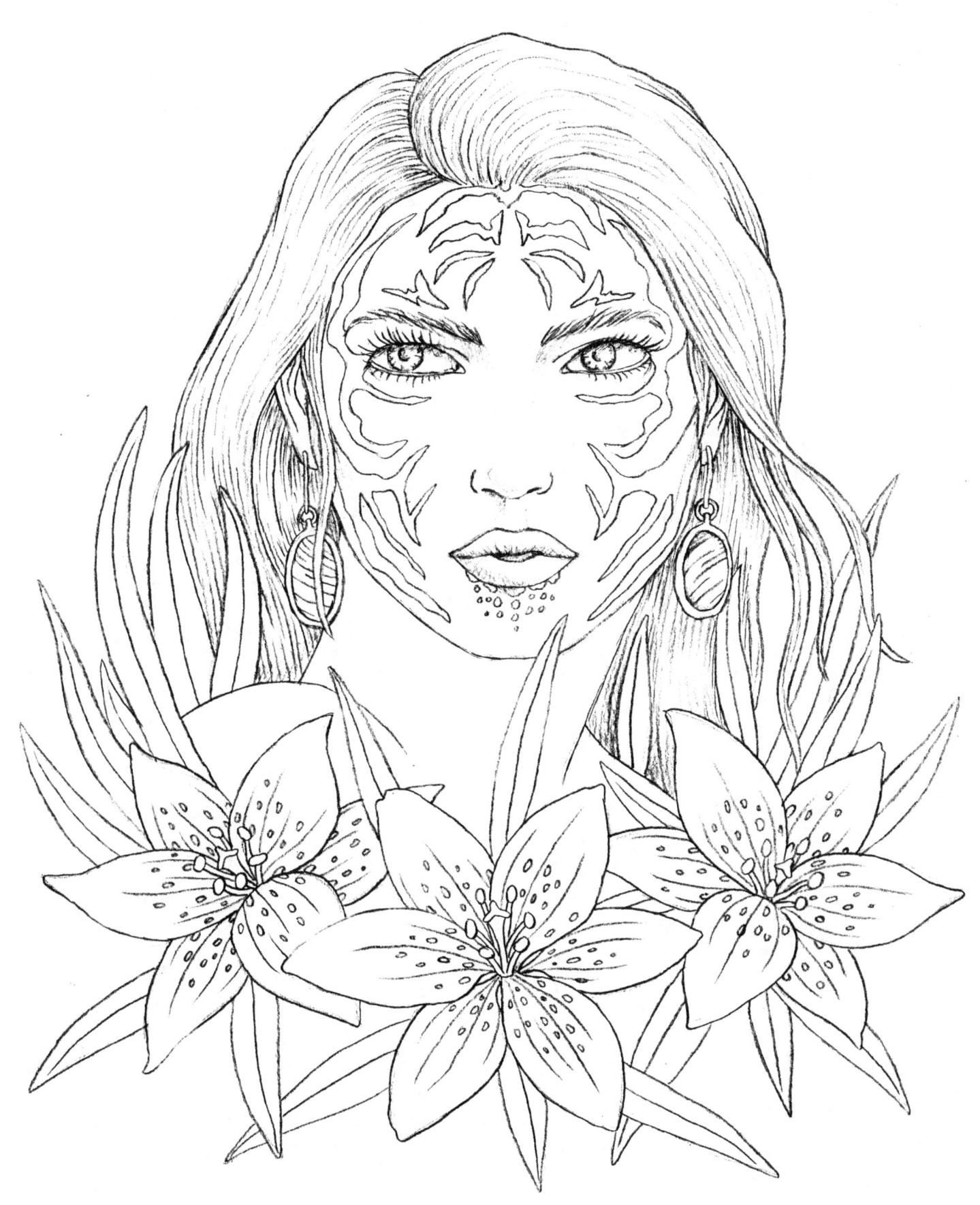

HARE

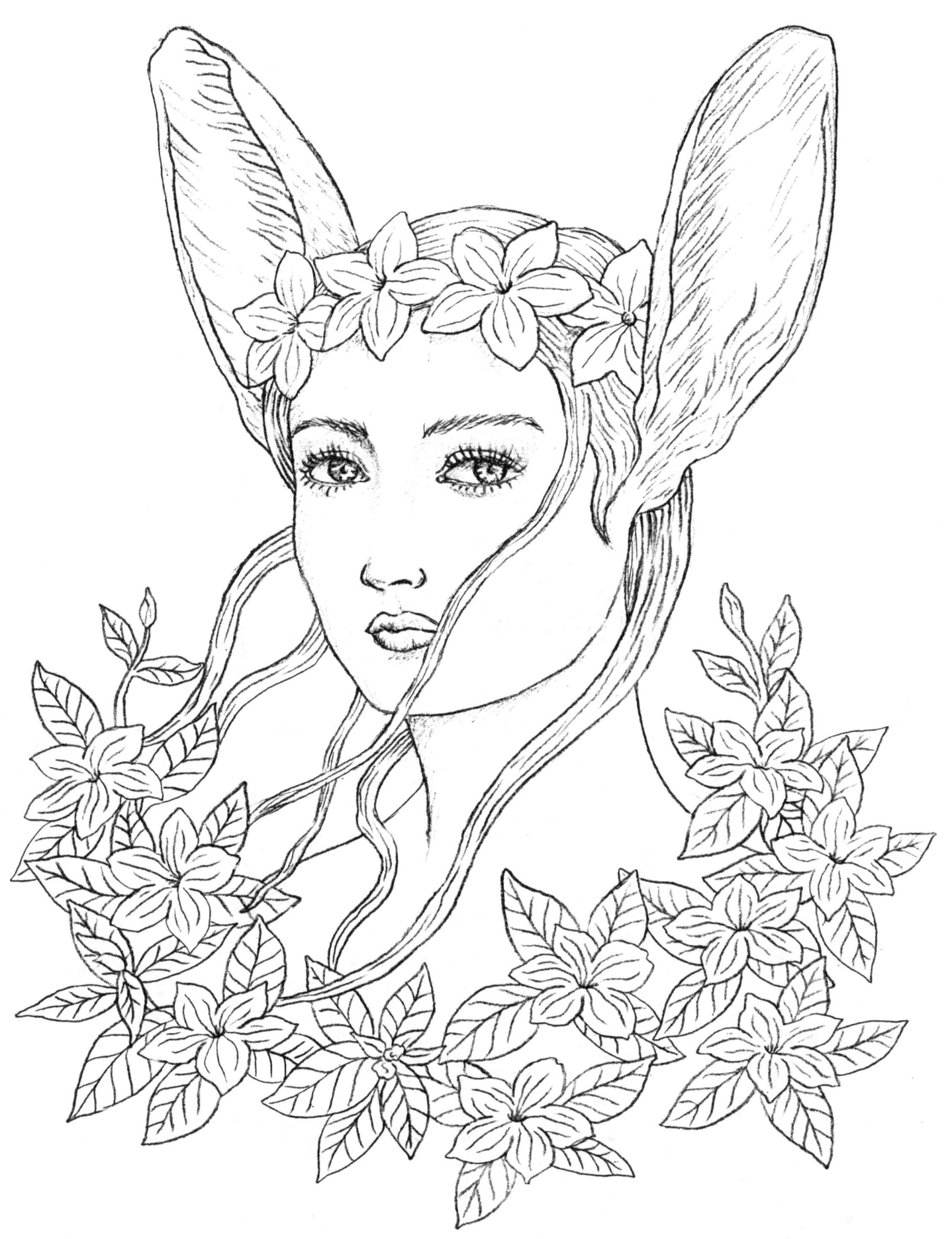

WATER BUFFALO

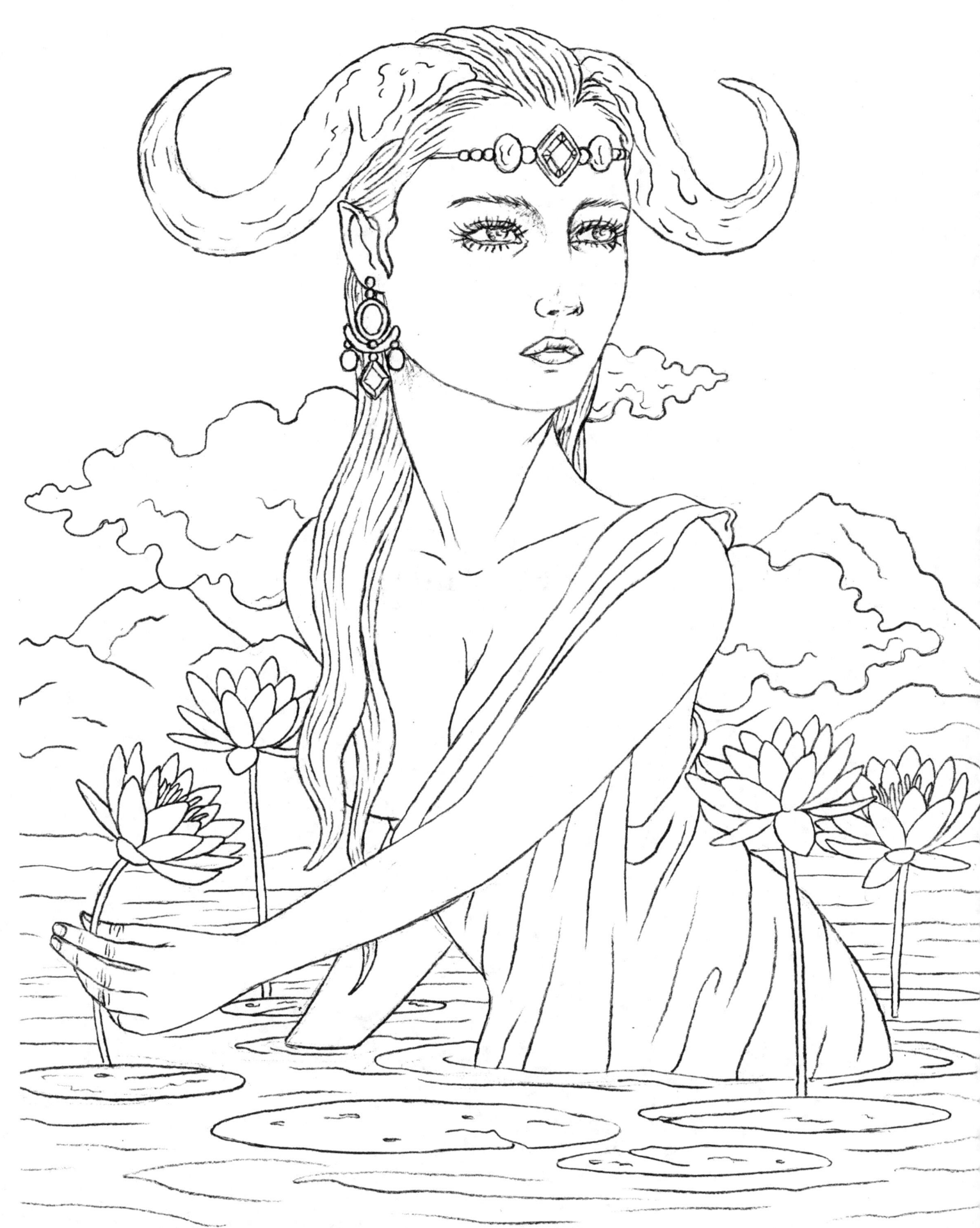

ELEPHANT

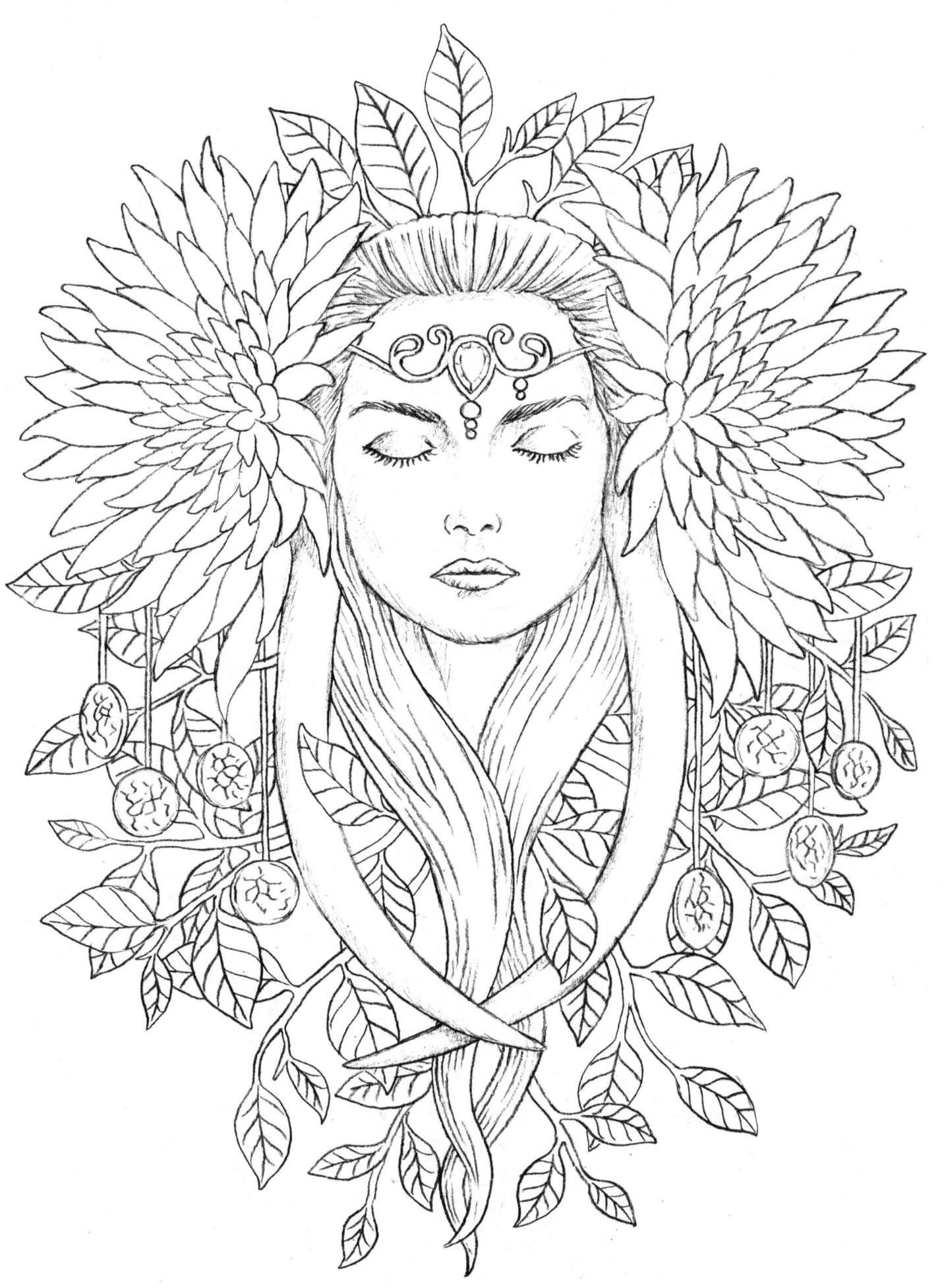

HORSE

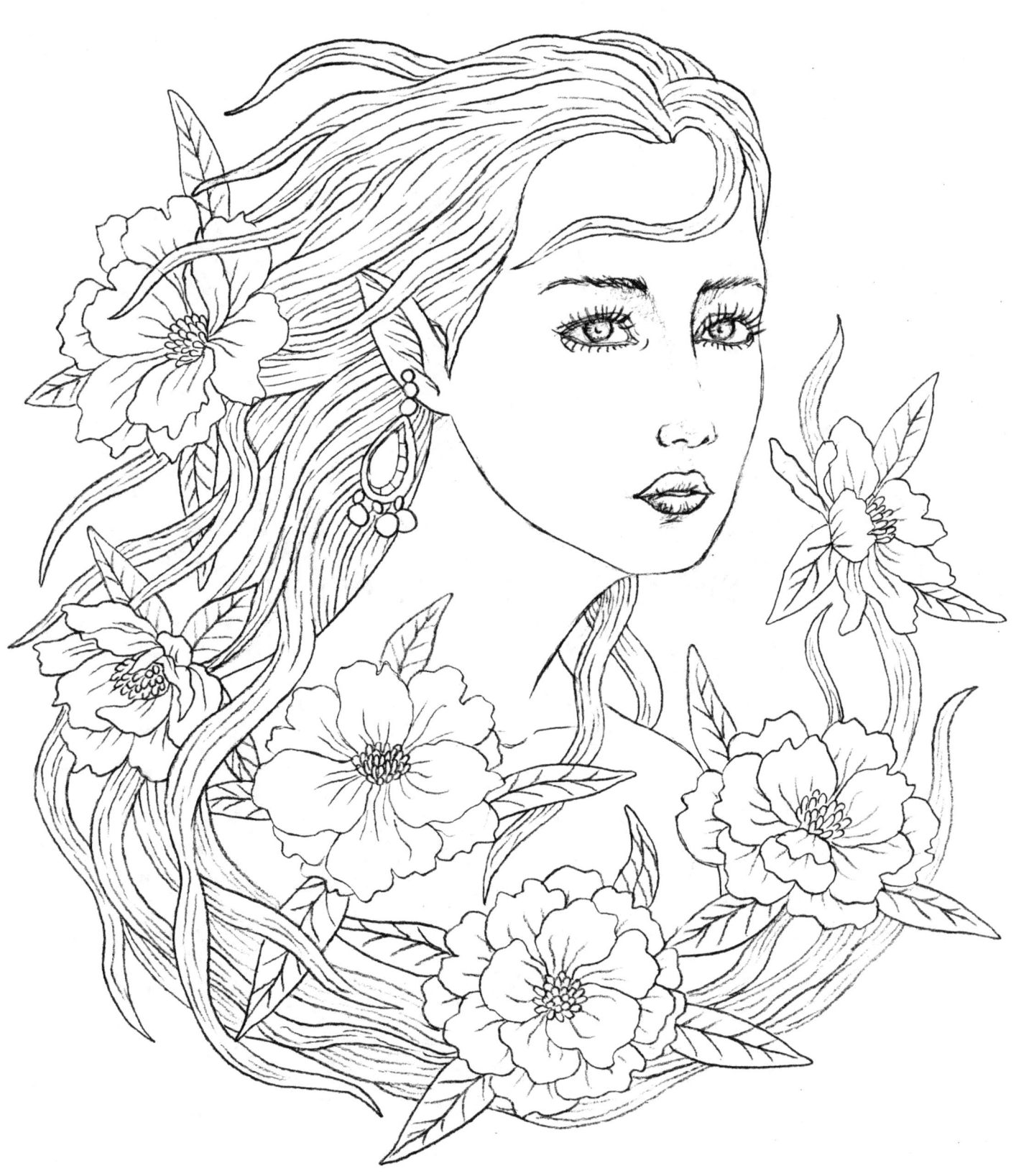

SIAMESE FIGHTING FISH

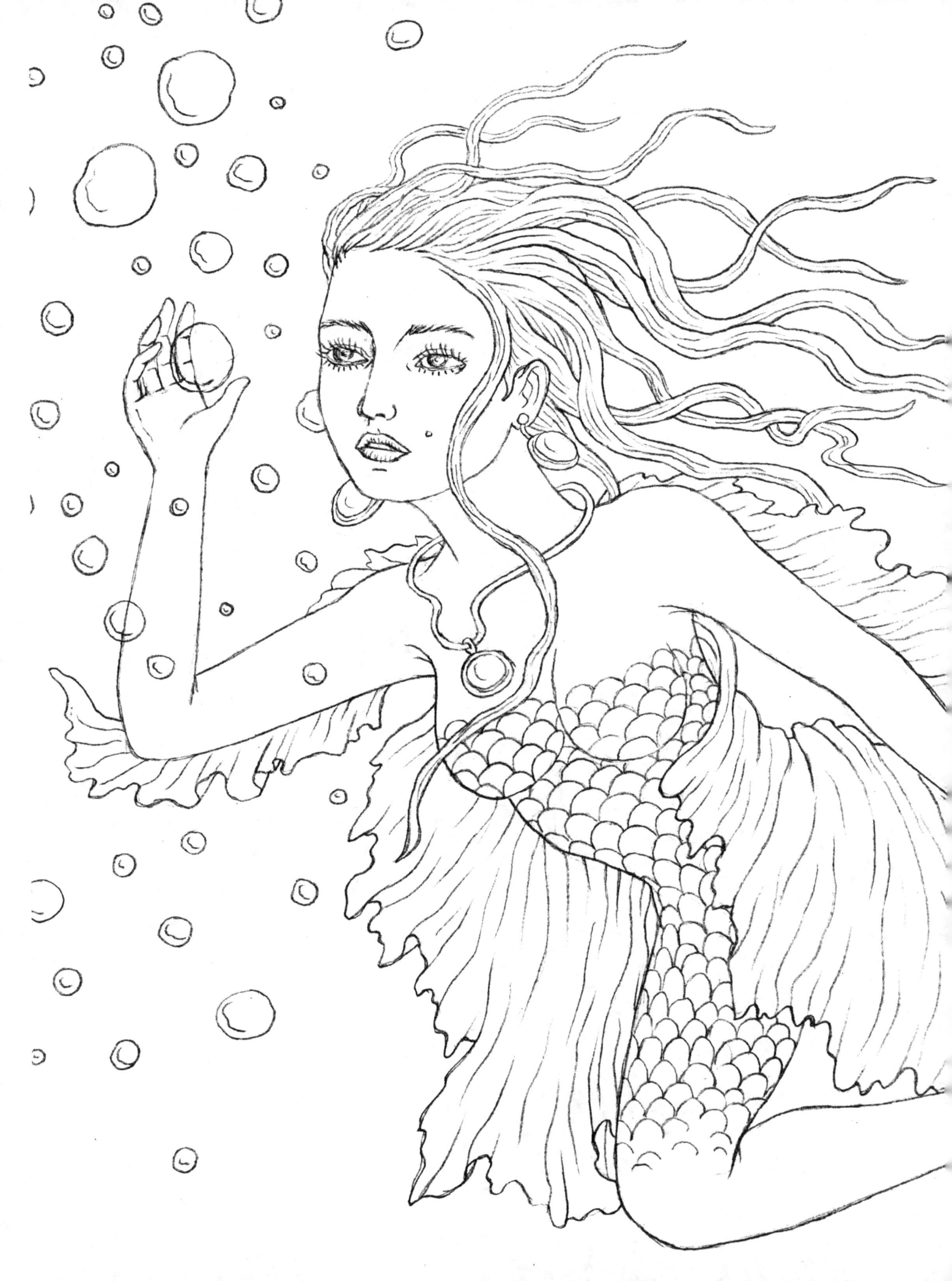

FENNEC FOX

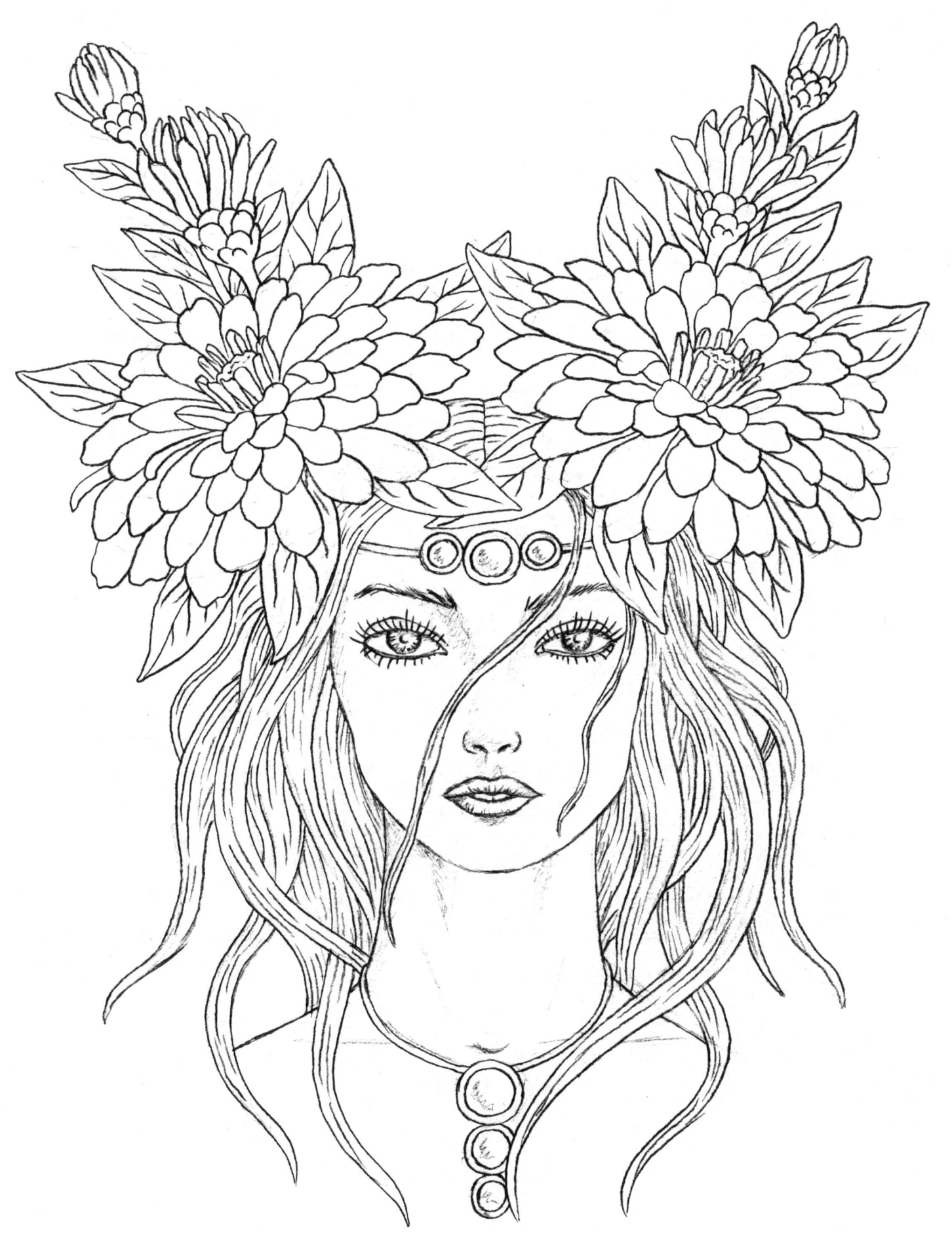

HOOPOE

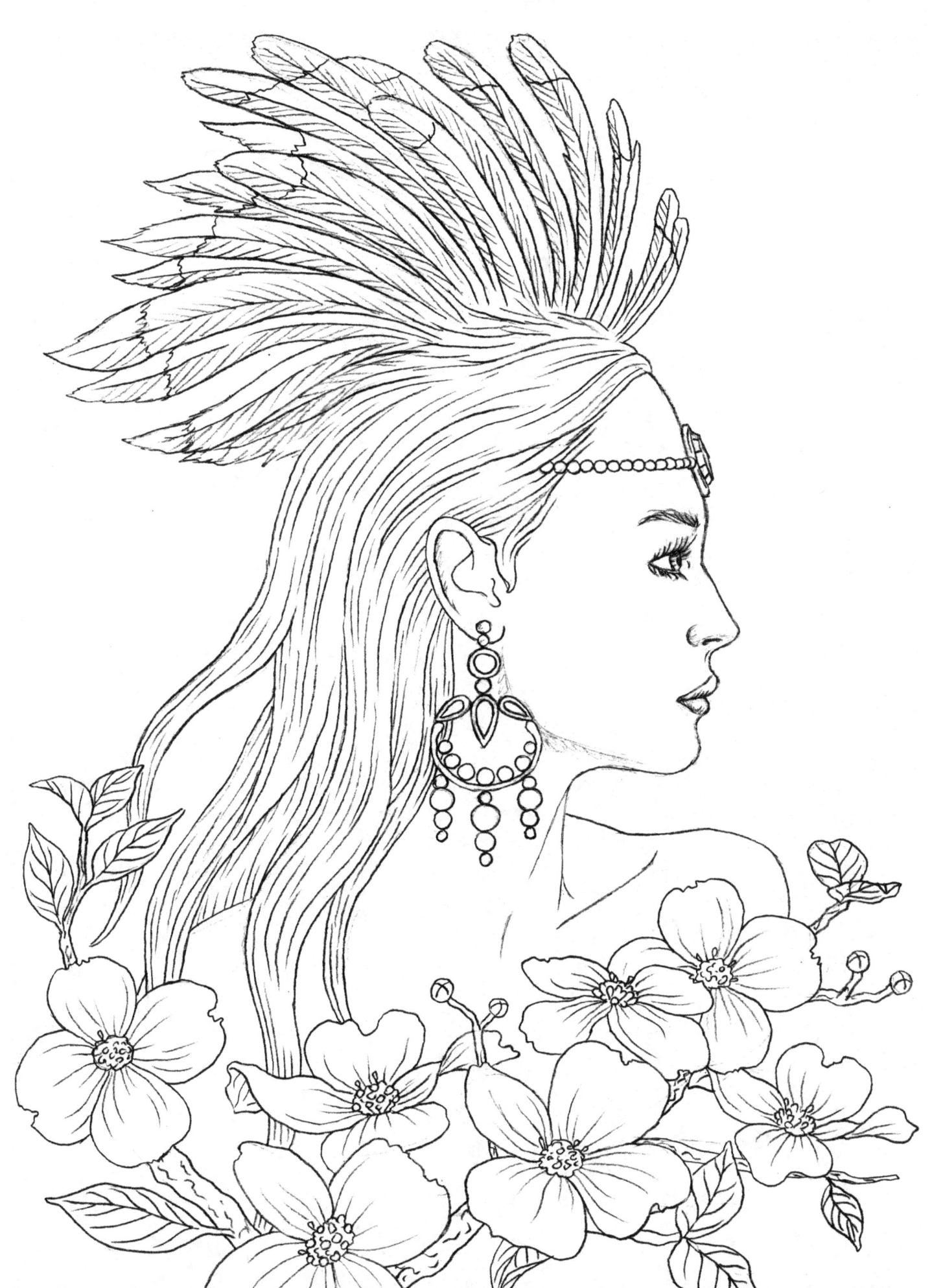

DEER

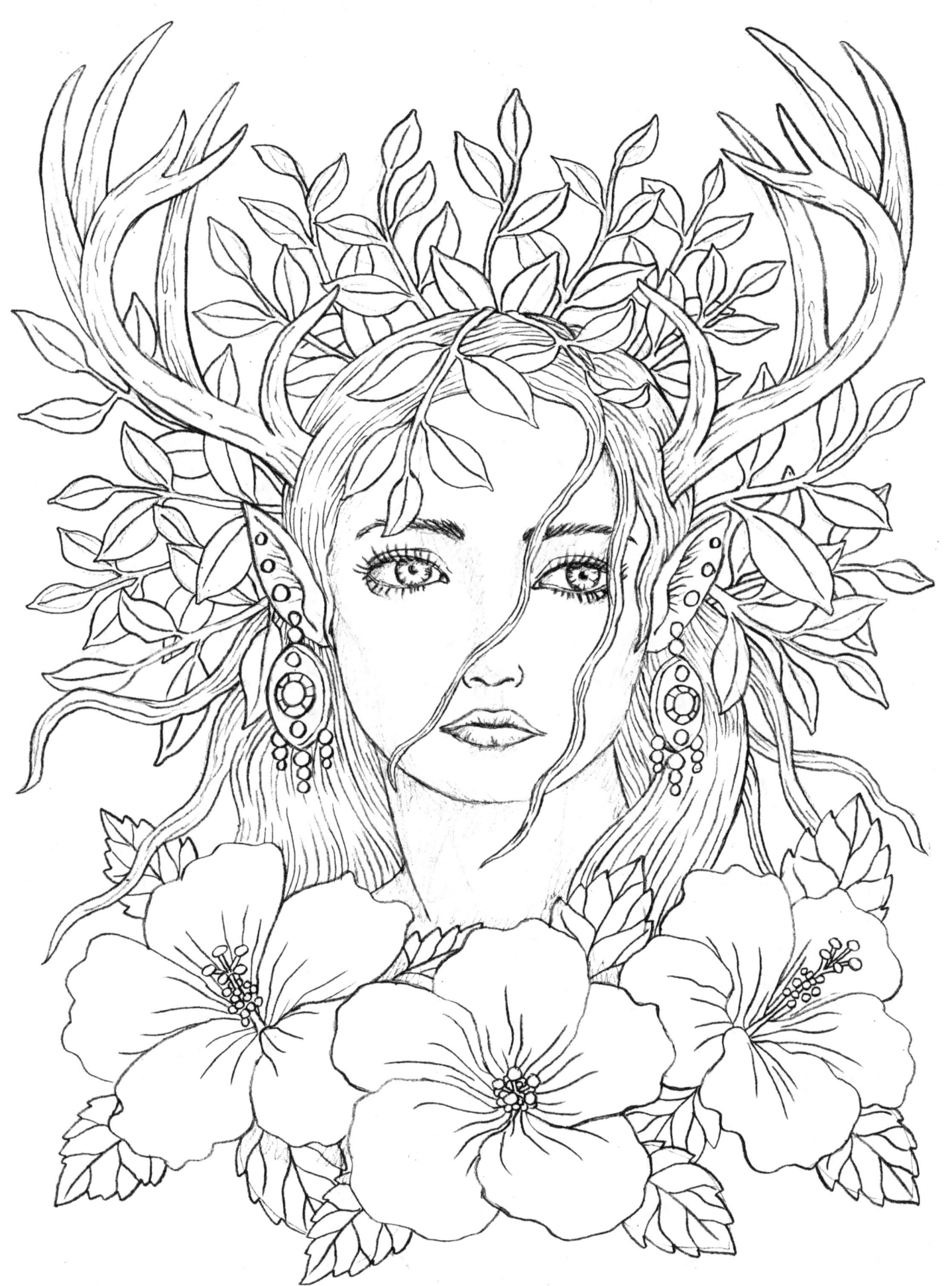

ALSO AVAILABLE FROM VIVID PUBLISHERS

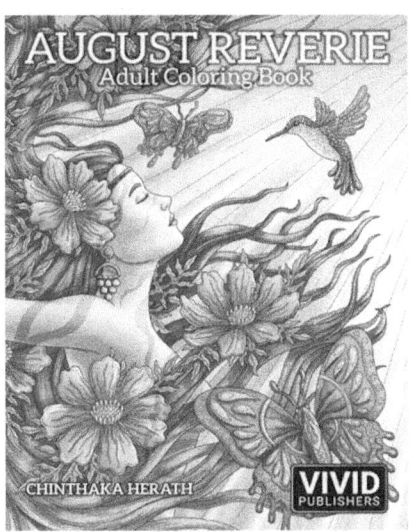

August Reverie

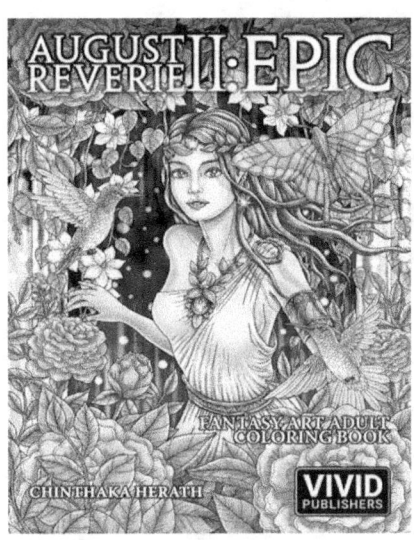

August Reverie 2: Epic

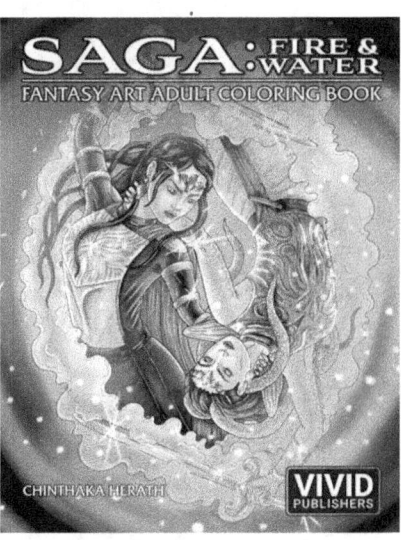

Saga: Fire & Water

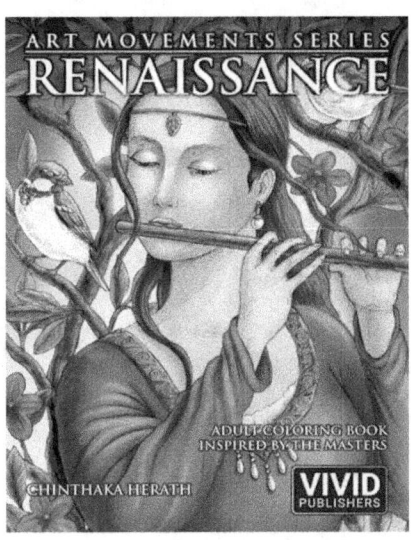

Art Movements Series: Renaissance

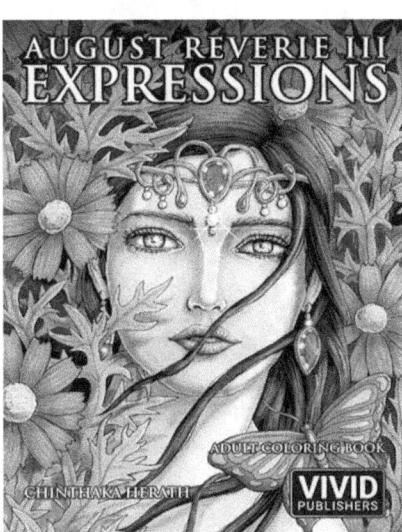

August Reverie 3: Expressions

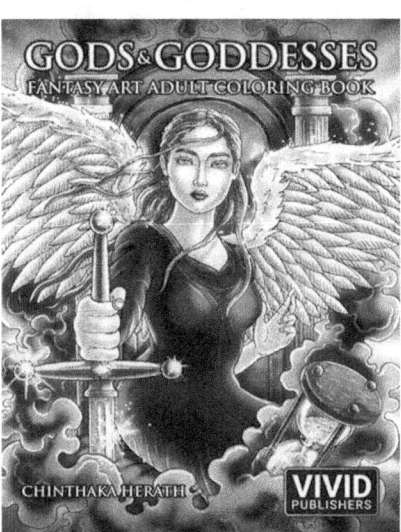

Gods & Goddesses

Preview all the pages at www.vividpublishers.com/books

www.ingramcontent.com/pod-product-compliance
Lightning Source LLC
Chambersburg PA
CBHW081657220526
45466CB00009B/2796